Name: _____

MW01242270

The
Campers

Completion of work: _____

Neatness: _____

Mastery of skills: _____

Pages _____ – not done in class.

Pages _____ – homework (in HW booklet)

Grade: 2
Volume: 1

Parents signature: _____

Reading

Name: _____   **Date:** _____

The Campers

It is Summer.

Sam, Pippin, Ronda…

Rumpus puts in a peg.

Sam mends the tent.

The tent gets fat.

Sam is sadder.

Name: _____   **Date:** _____

The Campers

It is Summer.

It is hot.

Sam, Pippin, Ronda, and Rumpus put up a tent.

Sam puts in a peg.

Pippin puts in a peg.

Ronda puts in a peg.

Rumpus puts in a peg.

Sam puts in a rod.

Pippin puts in a rod.

The tent sags.

Ronda tugs on the tent.

Rumpus tugs on the tent.

Ronda tugs hard.

Rumpus tugs harder.

The tent rips!

Sam mends the tent.

Sam gets in the tent. It is fun.

Name: _____ **Date:** _____

Story Mapping

Characters

_____
_____
_____
_____
_____
_____

Setting

_____
_____
_____
_____
_____
_____

What happened?

_____
_____
_____
_____
_____

At the end...

_____
_____

Phonics

Name: _____   **Date:** _____

Listen carefully as your teacher reads aloud the names of the boys in your class. Listen for the <u>beginning</u> sound in each name and mark that letter with a line in the chart below.

a	b	c	d	e	f	
g	h	i	j	k	l	
m	n	o	p	q	r	s
t	u	v	w	x	y	z

Now circle the letter that has the most lines.

The beginning sound most common in your class list is _____.

Name: _____   **Date:** _____

Listen carefully as your teacher reads aloud the names of the boys in your class. Listen for the <u>ending</u> sound in each name and mark that letter with a line, in the chart below.

a	b	c	d	e	f	
g	h	i	j	k	l	
m	n	o	p	q	r	s
t	u	v	w	x	y	z

Now circle the letter that has the most lines.

The ending sound most common in your class list is _____.

Name:

Date:

Can you think of words that end with the suffix /er/? Write them in the big /er/.

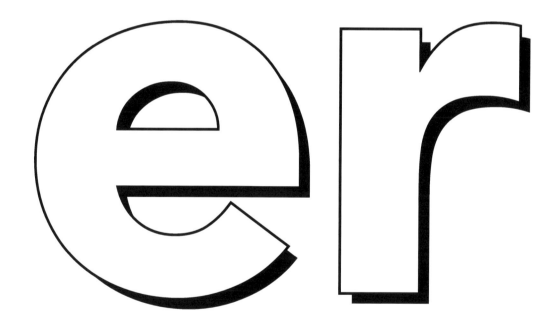

Name: _____　　**Date:** _____

Match the words to a phrase in the box. Write the numbers.

(1) summer

(2) hot

(3) sags

(4) Sam

(5) peg

(6) hard

(7) mend

(8) sadder

(9) saddest

(10) under

____ to fix

____ more sad

__1__ a season

____ opposite of over

____ opposite of cold

____ rhymes with card

____ the most sad

____ rhymes with leg

____ a character

____ rhymes with bags

Name: _____

Date: _____

Fill in the missing letters.

c _ar_____

st_____

b_____n

c_____d

st_____t

b_____

h_____p

y_____d

c_____pet

Name: _____   **Date:** _____

Draw a picture to show the meaning of the sentence. Underline the word that has the suffix **er**.

Chaim is big. **Tzvi is <u>bigger</u>.** 	**The water is cold.** **The soda is colder.**
Dovi is mad. **Yanky is madder.**	**Rabbit runs fast.** **Deer runs faster.**
A camel is tall. **A giraffe is taller.**	**At night it is dark.** **In my room it is darker.**

Name: _____   **Date:** _____

Fill in the missing word and the suffix used.

Phrase	Word	Suffix
more loud	louder	er
more small		
more low		
more sick		
more sad		
more fat		
more hard		

harder   lower   sicker
        fatter   sadder   smaller

The suffix er means _____.

Name: _____   **Date:** _____

Start the Show

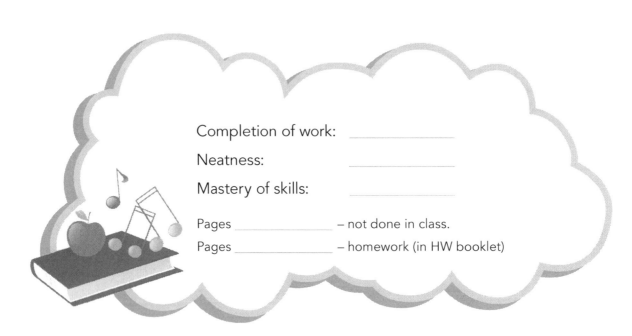

Completion of work: _____

Neatness: _____

Mastery of skills: _____

Pages _____ – not done in class.

Pages _____ – homework (in HW booklet)

Grade: 2
Volume: 2

Parents signature: _____

Reading

Name: _____

Date: _____

Words

hundred

monsters

dust ---------------------→ dusted

dart ---------------------→ darted

mend---------------------→ mended

hunt ---------------------→ hunted

drift ---------------------→ drifted

nod ---------------------→ nodded

show

Name: _____   **Date:** _____

Start The Show

One hundred monsters sat in the sun.

One hundred monsters met for fun.

Ten rag monsters dusted the stars.

Ten fast monsters darted in cars.

Ten sad monsters mended the huts. Ten red monsters hunted for nuts.

Ten fat monsters fed the cats. Ten smart monsters sat on mats.

Ten egg monsters drifted in cups. Ten hand monsters petted the pups.

Ten tin monsters tested a drum. Ten mop monsters started to hum.

One hundred monsters sat in the sun. One hundred monsters ended the fun.

One monster nodded to end the show. One hundred monsters got up to go.

Phonics

Name: _____

Date: _____

How many words can you think of with the suffix /ed/?
Write them in the big /ed/.

Name: _____　　**Date:** _____

Combine the root word and the suffix to make a new word.
Write it on the line.

Root Word	Suffix	Word
dust	ed	dusted
dart	ed	
mend	ed	
hunt	ed	
drift	ed	
test	ed	
start	ed	
end	ed	

Read the word at the end. Fill in the root word and the suffix.

Root Word	Suffix	Word
start	ed	started
		drifted
		ended
		tested
		hunted
		dusted

Name: _____   **Date:** _____

1-1-1 Rule

When you have a word with **1 syllable – 1 vowel** in the word – and **1 consonant** after the vowel, you double the consonant then add the suffix. (mop+ed=mopped)

Circle the words that are 1-1-1 words;

hunt

dust

pet

drift

nod

spot

fit

test

end

Add the suffix **ed** to those words and write them on the line. Don't forget to double the consonants.

_____   _____

_____   _____

Name: _____   **Date:** _____

Fun at Peg's

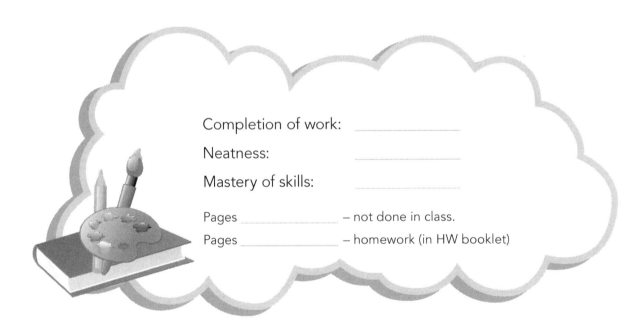

Completion of work: _____

Neatness: _____

Mastery of skills: _____

Pages _____ – not done in class.

Pages _____ – homework (in HW booklet)

Grade: 2
Volume: 3

Parents signature: _____

Reading

Name: _____

Date: _____

Fun At Peg's

The fun at Peg's had started.

He dipped in and got one out.

Amanda had a hard egg.

Pat handed it fast to Greg.

Scott pinned the hat on the cat.

Peg and Amanda passed the cups.

Name: _____   **Date:** _____

Fun at Peg's

The fun at Pegs had started.

Peg dropped apples into a pan.

Scott had to dip in and get an apple.

He dipped in and got one out.

Scott and the apple dripped.

Amanda had a hard egg.

Dad said, "Get set, go!"

Amanda passed the egg fast to Pat.

Pat handed it fast to Greg.

Greg started to pass the egg to Scott.

Greg missed.

He dropped the hard egg on the rug.

Peg handed Pat a hat and a pin.

Pat had to pin the hat on the cat.

Pat missed the cat.

She pinned the hat on the dog.

Pat handed Scott a hat and a pin.

Scott did it.

Scott pinned the hat on the cat.

Peg's mom and dad set out the dinner.

Peg and Amanda passed the cups.

After dinner Scott, Pat, Amanda, and Greg said, "Thanks, Peg."

Name: _____   **Date:** _____

Story Mapping

Characters   ### Setting

_____   _____

- - - - - - - - - - - - - - -   - - - - - - - - - - - - - - -

_____   _____

_____   _____

- - - - - - - - - - - - - - -   - - - - - - - - - - - - - - -

_____   _____

- - - - - - - - - - - - - - -   - - - - - - - - - - - - - - -

_____   _____

What happened?

_____

- -

_____

_____

- -

_____

At the end...

_____

- -

Phonics

Name: _____ **Date:** _____

Combine the root word and the suffix to make a new word. Write it on the line.

Root Word	Suffix	Word
drop	ed	dropped
dip	ed	
pass	ed	
dump	ed	
miss	ed	
pin	ed	
step	ed	
camp	ed	

Read the word at the end. Fill in the root word and the suffix.

Root Word	Suffix	Word
dump	ed	dumped
		camped
		missed
		pinned
		hugged
		dipped

Name: _____   **Date:** _____

1-1-1 Rule

When you have a word with **1 syllable – 1 vowel** in the word – and **1 consonant** after the vowel, you double the consonant then add the suffix. (mop+ed=mopped)

Circle the words that are 1-1-1 words;

dump

camp

pass

hug

wish

watch

dip

mop

pet

Add the suffix **ed** to those words and write them on the line. Don't forget to double the consonants.

_____   _____

_____   _____

Name: _____   **Date:** _____

Syllabication Review

One Syllable	Two Syllable
missed	ended

Sort the words by the amount of syllables they have, into the chart above.

ended	started	passed	mopped	petted
missed	grinned	handed	dipped	parted
darted	dropped	dumped	hugged	drifted

Name: _____   **Date:** _____

A Trip to the Stars

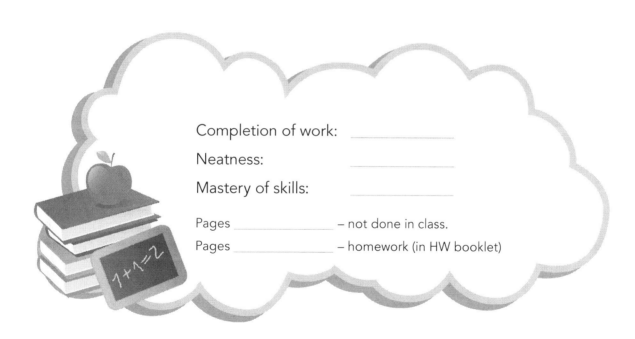

Completion of work: _____

Neatness: _____

Mastery of skills: _____

Pages _____ – not done in class.

Pages _____ – homework (in HW booklet)

Grade: 2
Volume: 4

Parents signature: _____

Reading

Name: _____   **Date:** _____

A Trip to the Stars

a carpet

on the grass

past a nest

Winston sat up

the wagon

"It's not far," said the farmer.

Name: _____   **Date:** _____

A Trip to the Stars

Winston put a carpet on the grass.
His dog ran up to him.
The dog and Winston rested on the carpet.
Winston and his dog had a nap.

The carpet started to go up.
It went past the garden.
The wind sent the carpet up past a nest.
The carpet went up faster and faster.

A farmer stopped.
"Is it far to the stars?" said Winston.

"It's not far," said the farmer.

"Thank you," said Winston.

The wagon and the carpet started to go fast.
"A trip to the stars is fun," said Winston.

"ARF! ARF!" said his dog.

The wind stopped.
Winston's carpet started to drop.
It went past the nest and past the garden.
The carpet dropped onto the grass.

Winston's dog got up.
It tugged on Winston's pants.

Winston sat up and hugged his dog.
His trip to the stars had ended.

Name: _____   **Date:** _____

Story Mapping

Characters	Setting

What happened?

At the end...

Phonics

Name: _____   **Date:** _____

Read through the root words and circle the 1-1-1 words. Then combine the root word and the suffix to make a new word. Don't forget to double the consonants of the 1-1-1 words you circled.

Root Word	Suffix	Word
rest	ed	rested
start	ed	
fast	er	
farm	er	
stop	ed	
star	s	
drop	ed	
tug	ed	

Read the word at the end. Fill in the root word and the suffix.

Root Word	Suffix	Word
end	ed	ended
		hugged
		stopped
		started
		farmer
		gardens

Name: _____　　　Date: _____

Syllabication Review

One Syllable	Two Syllable
grass	Winston

Sort the words by the amount of syllables they have, into the chart above.

Winston	carpet	grass	rested	started
garden	faster	farmer	stopped	stars
wagon	dropped	green	tugged	hugged

Name: _____   **Date:** _____

Blending Sheet

a	b	c	d	e	f	
g	h	i	j	k	l	
m	n	o	p	q	r	s
t	u	v	w	x	y	z

Name: _____   **Date:** _____

Match the word to a phrase in the box. Write the number.

(1) carpet

(2) dog

(3) Winston

(4) grass

(5) nap

(6) garden

(7) farmer

(8) wagon

(9) stars

(10) tugged

____ pulled

____ a short rest

____ someone who farms

____ a pet

____ the name of a boy

_1_ like a rug

____ it is green

____ where flowers grow

____ you can get a ride in it

____ in the sky at night

Name: _____ **Date:** _____

Smart Coppertop

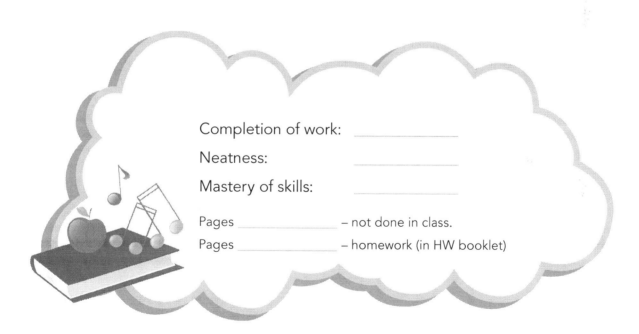

Completion of work: _____

Neatness: _____

Mastery of skills: _____

Pages _____ – not done in class.

Pages _____ – homework (in HW booklet)

**Grade: 2
Volume: 5**

Parents signature: _____

Reading

Name: _____   Date: _____

Smart Coppertop

Marta

Coppertop is a smart pet.

can harm a garden

on the steps

to wet the garden

western hat

Name: _____   **Date:** _____

Smart Coppertop

Marta has a pet hen.
Her hen is Coppertop.
Coppertop is a smart pet.

Marta has started a garden.
Coppertop can't go into the garden.
A hen can harm a garden.
Coppertop sits on the steps.

The sun is hot.
Marta must get her garden wet.
She gets a can to wet the garden.

Coppertop sees Marta.
Coppertop sees the garden.
She runs into the garden.

Marta drops the can and runs after her!

Coppertop runs under Marta's wagon.
Marta runs after her.
Marta's western hat drops off.

A wind starts up.
It huffs and puffs.
The wind has Marta's hat.

Name: _____   **Date:** _____

The hat is up, up, up.
"Stop, hat, stop!" said Marta.

The hat stops on a twig.
Marta can't get it.
"Get the hat, Coppertop!"
"It's on the twig," said Marta.
Coppertop hops up on the twig.
The hen tugs and tugs on the hat.
The hat drops off the twig.

"Thank you," said Marta.
"You did it!"

Name: _____   **Date:** _____

Story Mapping

Characters

_____

- -

_____

_____

_____

- -

_____

Setting

_____

- -

_____

_____

_____

- -

_____

What happened?

_____

- -

_____

_____

- -

_____

At the end...

_____

- -

Phonics

Name: _____   **Date:** _____

Sort the words on the bottom of the page by syllables.

One Syllable	Two Syllable
drops	Marta

Sort the words by the amount of syllables they have, into the chart above.

Marta	garden	started	into
after	under	western	twig
drops	start	thank	you

Name: _____   **Date:** _____

Blending Sheet

a	b	c	d	e	f	
g	h	i	j	k	l	
m	n	o	p	q	r	s
t	u	v	w	x	y	z

Name: _____   **Date:** _____

Match the word with a phrase from the box. Write the number.

(1) carpet

(2) Marta

(3) smart

(4) start

(5) harm

(6) garden

(7) farmer

(8) barn

(9) stars

(10) car

____ rhymes with farm

_1_ like a rug

____ someone who farms

____ rhymes with start

____ the name of a girl

____ a house for horses

____ begin

____ where flowers grow

____ you can get a ride in it

____ in the sky at night

Name: _____   **Date:** _____

Watson's Camp

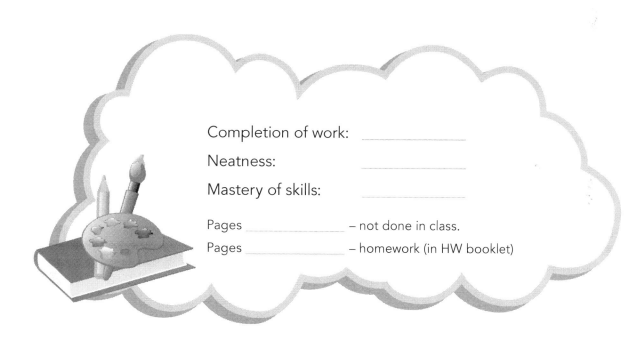

Completion of work: _____

Neatness: _____

Mastery of skills: _____

Pages _____ – not done in class.

Pages _____ – homework (in HW booklet)

Grade: 2
Volume: 6

Parents signature: _____

Reading

Name: _____   **Date:** _____

Watson's Camp

Watson was sad

"Emma gets to swim..."

"I want a tent"

"Grandma wants to see you"

to the farm

grinned

Name: _____   **Date:** _____

Watson's Camp

It was summer.
Watson was sad.
His sister Emma was at camp.
Watson wanted to go to camp, too.

"I want to swim," said Watson.
"Emma gets to swim at camp."

"I want to pump water," said Watson.
"Emma gets to pump water at camp."

"I want a tent," said Watson.
"Emma gets a tent at camp."

"I want to go to camp," said Watson.

"You get to go to the farm," said Dad.
"Grandma wants to see you."

"The farm is not camp!" said Watson.
"Emma got to go to camp."

Watson went to the farm.
Grandma showed Watson the farm.
She showed him the pond.

Name: _____ **Date:** _____

"You can swim in the pond, if you want to," said Grandma.

She showed him the pump.
"You can pump water for us, if you want to," said Grandma.

She showed him a tent.
"You can put up the tent, if you want to ," said Grandma.

Grandma showed Watson her dog Snuff.
Snuff had pups!
Grandma handed Watson a tan pup.

"The tan pup is for you, if you want it," she said.

"The farm is fun!" said Watson.

Watson hugged his pup and grinned.
"Thank you, Grandma."

"I got a pup at the farm," he said.
"Emma can't get a pup at camp!"

Name: _____ **Date:** _____

Story Mapping

Characters	Setting

What happened?

_____

_____

_____

_____

_____

At the end...

_____

_____

Name: _____   **Date:** _____

1. What were the things that Emma got to do at camp?

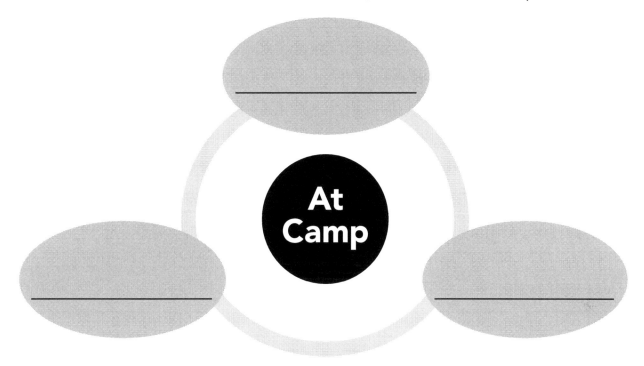

2. What were the things that Watson got to do on the farm?

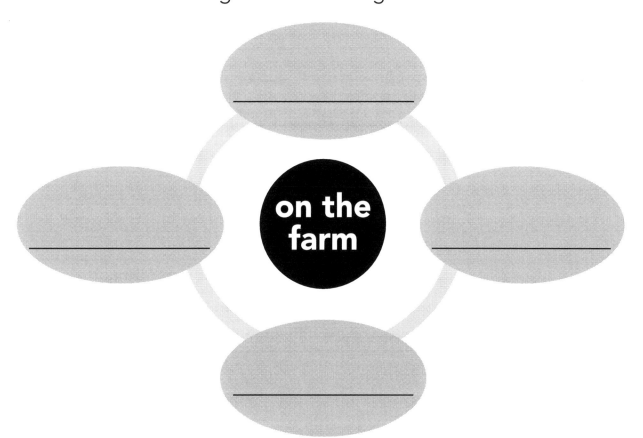

Phonics

Name: _____   **Date:** _____

Sort the words on the bottom of the page by syllables.

One Syllable	Two Syllable
camp	summer

Sort the words by the amount of syllables they have, into the chart above.

summer	Watson	sister	wanted
camp	swim	Emma	pump
water	farm	tent	Grandma

Name: _____ **Date:** _____

Match the words on the right with a phrase on the left. Write the numbers.

(1) was

(2) wanted

(3) Watson

(4) water

(5) summer

(6) sad

(7) swan

(8) swap

(9) camp

(10) pup

____ you can drink it

____ to switch

____ a beautiful duck

____ a fun place for kids

____ the name of a boy

____ a baby dog

____ it has an added suffix

_1_ the opposite of is

____ a season

____ the opposite of happy

Name: _____ **Date:** _____

Sight Word Review

Use the sight words to fill in the missing blanks.

go	play	my
find	funny	red
run	makes	It

I like to _____ at the park! I _____ to the

park with _____ mom. It _____ me laugh

when she pushes me up and down on the swing. It is

_____! I like to _____ as fast as I can

across the green grass. I look under a rock. I _____ a

bug hiding there. _____ is the color _____.

Name: _____   **Date:** _____

Blending Sheet

a	b	c	d	e	f	
g	h	i	j	k	l	
m	n	o	p	q	r	s
t	u	v	w	x	y	z

Name: _____   **Date:** _____

The Ants

It Warns You

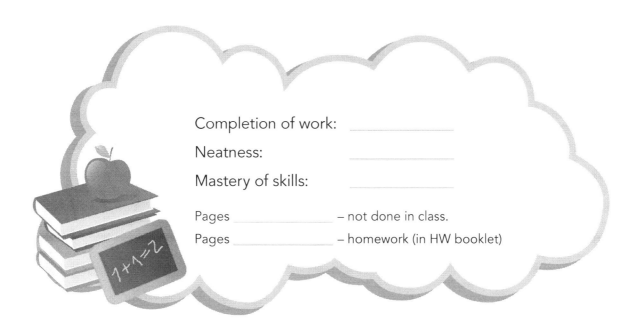

Completion of work: _____

Neatness: _____

Mastery of skills: _____

Pages _____ – not done in class.

Pages _____ – homework (in HW booklet)

Grade: 2
Volume: 7

Parents signature: _____

Name: _____   **Date:** _____

The Ants

a camper's arm

on a farm

ants dart

across the farmer's hand

a show

ants swim in the water

Name: _____   **Date:** _____

The Ants

1 ant runs up a camper's arm.

2 ants pump the water on a farm.

3 ants sit in the hot sun and sand.

4 ants dart across the farmer's hand.

5 ants wave and go to a show.

6 ants are sad. The ants want to go!

7 ants go on a summer trip.

8 ants swim in the water and drip.

Fill in the rhyming Pairs:

arm　———————————▶　_____

sand　———————————▶　_____

show　———————————▶　_____

trip　———————————▶　_____

Name: _____   **Date:** _____

1.   What were some things that the ants did?

_____

_____

_____

Ants

_____

_____

_____

Name: _____   **Date:** _____

It Warns You

This [   ] warns you not to go.

This [   ] warns cars not to go fast.

The [   ] warns you to stop.

The [   ] warns you to stop.

The [   ] warns you it must go fast!

Use the reader to help you fill in the blanks with the right street signs.

Name: _____　　　**Date:** _____

What are some things that different street signs warn about?

_____

_____

_____

_____

It
Warns
You

_____

_____

_____

Phonics

Name: _____   **Date:** _____

Sort the words on the bottom of the page by syllables.

One Syllable	Two Syllable
arm	camper

Sort the words by the amount of syllables they have, into the chart above.

camper	arm	sand	across
farmer	dart	wave	show
go	water	drip	want

Name: _____ **Date:** _____

Blending Sheet

a	b	c	d	e	f	
g	h	i	j	k	l	
m	n	o	p	q	r	s
t	u	v	w	x	y	z

Name: _____   **Date:** _____

r<u>u</u>ns

camp

arm

sand

ant

dart

farm

hand

pump

want

> 1. Underline the vowel in each word- and say the vowel sound (ar- should be read as one unit).
>
> 2. Read from the vowel till the end.
>
> 3. Read the whole word.

Name: _____   **Date:** _____

<u>war</u>n

war

warm

wart

swarm

warmer

1. Underline the chunk / <u>war</u> / and read it.

2. Read the chunk till the end.

3. Then add the beginning sound if there is one, and read.

4. Read the whole word.

Name: _____   Date: _____

Sight Word Review

Use the sight words to fill in the missing blanks.

where	you	it
find	help	Here
in	little	up

Sam has a new baby brother. Sam is big, but the baby is

_____. Sam likes to _____ his mom and

dad take care of the baby.

Mom says " _____ is the baby's blanket?"

Sam looks for _____. He wants to _____

the blanket to help his mom.

"_____ is the blanket, mom", says Sam. "It was

_____ the baby's crib. I went _____ the

stairs to his room to get it."

"Thank _____, Sam", says mom. "You are a good big

brother!"

Spelling

Name: _____   **Date:** _____

Spelling

short ă words;

1. man

_____

2. plan

_____

3. ran

_____

4. tan

_____

5. sand

_____

6. can

_____

Extra Credit;

1. the

_____

2. to

_____

Name: _____   **Date:** _____

Spelling Pre-Test

1. _____

_____

2. _____

_____

3. _____

_____

4. _____

_____

5. _____

_____

6. _____

_____

<u>Extra Credit</u>;

7. _____

_____

8. _____

_____

Name: _____   **Date:** _____

Spelling Review Sheet

Word Box

man   plan   ran   tan   sand   can   to   The

Fill in the missing word.

1. I like to play in a _____ box at the park.

2. Two, too, and _____ all sound the same.

3. The first _____ on earth was called Adam.

4. The deer _____ in front of my car.

5. If you sit in the sun you can get a sun _____.

6. I got a _____ of soda on the trip.

7. We have a fun _____ for the siyum party.

8. _____ siyum will be on Monday.

Name: _____   **Date:** _____

Spelling Review Sheet

Word Box

man	plan	ran	tan	sand	can	to	The

Fill in the blanks with words that rhyme from the spelling list.
Then think of your own rhyming words.

rhyme	spelling word	your own rhyme
ban		
fan		
clan		
nan		
dan		
hand		
new		
zebra		

Name: _____   **Date:** _____

Spelling Review Sheet

Word Box

man   plan   ran   tan   sand   can   to   the

Correct the spelling mistakes.

1. A **mann** came to fix our house. _____

2. We **pln** to have a big Chanukah party at our house. _____

3. The little boy **rann** after the bird. _____

4. My mother drives a **tn** colored van. _____

5. We have lots of **send** in our back yard. _____

6. I **kan** ride my big brother's bike. _____

7. I ride on a yellow bus **too** school every day. _____

8. I will sit in a seat with my friend on **thu** bus. _____

Name: _____   **Date:** _____

Paw Prints on the Steps

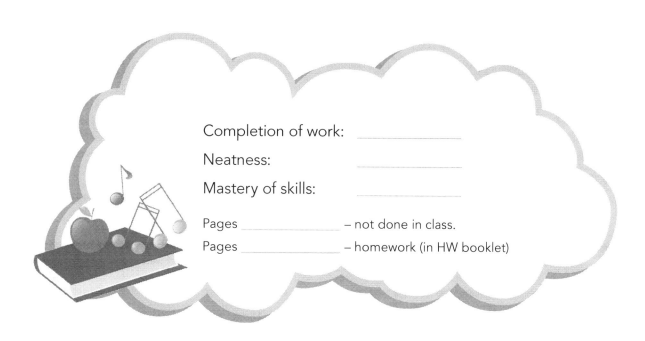

Completion of work: _____

Neatness: _____

Mastery of skills: _____

Pages _____ – not done in class.

Pages _____ – homework (in HW booklet)

Grade: 2
Volume: 8

Parents signature: _____

Reading

Name: _____   Date: _____

Paw Prints on the Steps

Mr. Ward

to the apartment

paw prints

Did a monster wander in?

mud on its paws

a gift for Dennis and Fran

Name: _____   **Date:** _____

Paw Prints on the Steps

Fran and Dennis run to the apartment.

They stop at the steps.

Dennis sees mud on the steps.

Fran sees paw prints.

The paw prints go up the steps.

Did a monster wander in?

Dennis and Fran run up the steps.

They run to Mr. Ward.

He has a mop in his hand.

"Did you see a monster go past?" said Fran.

"Is it in the apartment?" said Dennis.

Mr. Ward grinned.

"I didn't see it," he said.

"I must mop up the mess."

The paw prints go on up the steps.

Dennis and Fran must warn Mom.

Fran and Dennis run up the steps.

They stop at the top.

The wet paw prints go on and on.

Name: _____   **Date:** _____

The monster is in the apartment!

Did the monster harm Mom?

Can the monster harm us?

Fran and Dennis run into the apartment.

The monster is in the apartment.

It is a dog.

It has mud on its paws!

The monster is Moppet.

Moppet is a gift for Dennis and Fran.

They thank Mom and hug her.

They hug Moppet the monster, too!

Name: _____   **Date:** _____

Story Mapping

Characters	Setting

What happened?

_____

_____

_____

_____

_____

At the end...

_____

_____

Phonics

Name: _____   **Date:** _____

Sort the words on the bottom of the page by syllables.

One Syllable	Two Syllable
Fran	Dennis

Dennis	Fran	steps	monster
wander	Ward	grinned	warn
into	Moppet	gift	thank

Circle the words that are names of characters. What is different about those words? _____

Name: _____   **Date:** _____

Blending Sheet

a	b	c	d	e	f	
g	h	i	j	k	l	
m	n	o	p	q	r	s
t	u	v	w	x	y	z

Name: _____　　　**Date:** _____

____ s<u>aw</u>

____ raw

_1_ paw

____ draw

____ straw

____ straws

____ fawn

____ dawn

____ claw

____ law

> 1. Underline the chunk /aw/ and read it.
> 2. Then read the chunk till the end.
> 3. Add the beginning sound, and read.
> 4. Then read the whole word.

Read the clues below. Match them to the words on the left. Write the numbers.

1. The hand of a cat can be called a ____paw____.
2. A young deer is called a _____.
3. _____ is the part of the morning that the sun comes up.
4. A vegetable before it is cooked is _____.
5. It is fun to drink from a soda can with a _____.
6. My brother likes to drink from a soda can with two _____.
7. My older sister knows how to _____ people.
8. A _____ can be used to chop wood.
9. The squirrel dug a hole in the ground with its _____.
10. There is a _____ that one must wear a seatbelt in the car.

Name: _____   **Date:** _____

Draw a line to the /aw/ if the picture is spelled with an /aw/.

Write the /aw/ words on the lines.

_____   _____

_____   _____

_____   _____

_____   _____

Name: _____   **Date:** _____

1. pr**i**nt

2. steps

3. hand

4. m**u**st

5. grinned

6. stop

7. monster

8. Moppet

9. gift

1. Underline the vowel in each word- and say the vowel sound. If there are two syllables read one at a time.

2. Read from the vowel till the end.

3. Read the whole word.

Match the words on the left with a word or phrase from the box. Write the numbers.

_____ end

_____ a body part

_____1_____ to write

_____ smiled

_____ present

_____ have to

_____ a ladder

_____ a name

_____ something big and scary looking

Name: _____   **Date:** _____

Sight Word Review

Use the sight words to fill in the missing words.

a	and	away
big	blue	can
come	down	for

Rex _____ his family live in a _____ house. His

grandma and grandpa live far _____. It _____ take

them ten hours to drive over to Rex's house. They like to

_____ and visit. They will sleep in the guest room.

The guest room is _____ in the basement.

Next week they will come _____ Rex's birthday.

Grandma will bake _____ cake in the shape of a car.

She will bring a _____ present for Rex. Mom will

take lots of pictures.

Spelling

B
A
C

Name: _____   **Date:** _____

Spelling

short ĭ words;

1. pin

2. swim

3. rim

4. skin

5. tin

6. dim

Extra Credit;

1. is

2. go

Name: _____   **Date:** _____

Spelling Pre-Test

1. _____

2. _____

3. _____

4. _____

5. _____

6. _____

Extra Credit;

7. _____

8. _____

Name: _____   **Date:** _____

Spelling Review Sheet

Word Box

pin   swim   rim   skin   tin   dim   is   go

Fill in the missing word;

1. A room with little light is a _____ room.

2. In the summer I like to _____ in a pool every day.

3. Another word for the edge is the _____.

4. My baby has a red rash on her soft _____.

5. A sharp _____ fell on the floor.

6. We _____ to Boro Park for Rosh Hashana.

7. _____ is a type of metal.

8. This month _____ Kislev.

Name: _____   **Date:** _____

Spelling Review Sheet

Word Box

pin   swim   rim   skin   tin   dim   is   go

Fill in the blanks with words that rhyme from the spelling list.
Then think of your own rhyming words.

rhyme	spelling word	your own rhyme
win		
trim		
him		
grim		
fin		
bin		
his		
show		

Name: _____　　　　**Date:** _____

Spelling Review Sheet

Word Box

| pin | swim | rim | skin | tin | dim | is | go |

Correct the spelling mistakes.

1. The **pn** stuck to the wall. _____

2. It is not safe to **siwm** alone. _____

3. The girl stood on the **rimm** of the steps. _____

4. The pin made a red scratch on my **skn**. _____

5. The cake will bake in a **tinn** pan. _____

6. The lights grew **dimm** before the blackout hit. _____

7. Today **iz** my birthday. _____

8. We will **gow** to the pizza shop for supper on my birthday.

_____

Name: _____   **Date:** _____

The Flag

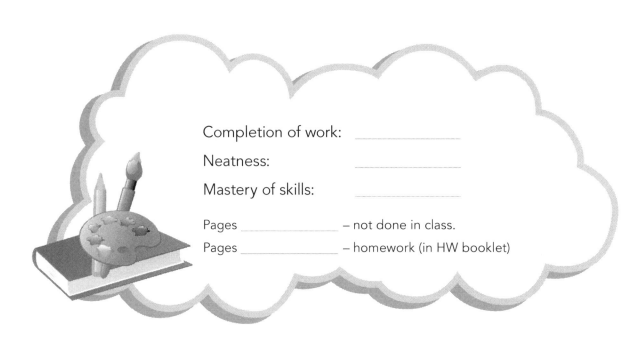

Completion of work: _____

Neatness: _____

Mastery of skills: _____

Pages _____ – not done in class.

Pages _____ – homework (in HW booklet)

Grade: 2
Volume: 9

Parents signature: _____

Reading

Name: _____   **Date:** _____

The Flag

Sam, Pippin, Ronda, and Rumpus

"A star has tips,"…

"I want to draw different stars"…

Sam handed the flag to Ronda.

It flapped and fluttered.

"It is a grand flag!"

Name: _____　　　**Date:** _____

The Flag

Sam, Pippin, Ronda, and Rumpus wanted a flag.

"I can draw it," said Sam.

"Can you draw stars?" said Rumpus.

"Draw stars," said Pippin.

"Yes, draw stars!" said Ronda.

Sam started to draw a star.

"Show us the star!" said Rumpus.

Sam held it up.

"No, no," said Ronda.

"A star has tips," said Pippin.
"You must add tips."

Sam started to draw tips.

"Now show us the star," said Rumpus.

Sam held it up.

"No, no," said Ronda.
"Now the star has lumps!" said Pippin.

Name: _____

Date: _____

"A star is hard to draw," said Sam.

"I want to draw different stars," said Sam.
Sam started to draw.

"Let us see the flag," said Rumpus.

"Not now," said Sam.

"I want to see the flag!" said Pippin.

"Not now," said Sam.

"Show us the flag," said Ronda.

"You can see it now," said Sam.

Sam handed the flag to Ronda.
She held the flag up.
It flapped and fluttered in the wind.

"You put us on the flag!" said Rumpus.

"Yes," said Sam.
"I put the top stars on the flag."

"It is a grand flag!" said Pippin.

"It is a flag of stars!" said Ronda.

And it was.

Name: _____ **Date:** _____

Story Mapping

Characters	Setting

What happened?

At the end...

Phonics

Name: _____   **Date:** _____

Sort the words on the bottom of the page by syllables.

One Syllable	Two Syllable	Three Syllable
draw	Pippin	

Pippin	Ronda	Rumpus	wanted
started	draw	star	show
different	handed	flag	flapped

Circle the words that are names of characters. What is different about those words? _____

Name: _____ **Date:** _____

Blending Sheet

a	b	c	d	e	f	
g	h	i	j	k	l	
m	n	o	p	q	r	s
t	u	v	w	x	y	z

Name: _____   **Date:** _____

___ left

___ list

___ lost

___ lift

___ plan

_1_ plant

___ clap

___ help

___ held

1. Underline the vowel in each word and say the vowel sound. If there are two syllables read one at a time.

2. Read from the vowel till the end.

3. Read the whole word.

Read the clues below. Match them to the words on the left. Write the numbers.

1. A _____ needs water and sunlight to grow.

2. At the end of the play you must _____ really hard.

3. I _____ my homework at home this morning.

4. It is good to _____ someone in any way that you can.

5. My mother has a _____ of all the boys in my class and their phone numbers.

6. The little boy was crying when he _____ his red candy.

7. My mother _____ the crying baby for two hours.

8. I like to _____ the challah cover to smell the challahs before the meal.

9. We will _____ a trip to the zoo during our Spring break.

Name: _____   **Date:** _____

Sight Word Review

Use the sight words to fill in the missing words.

I	is	jump	look
me	not	one	said
see	yellow	the	

Dovid _____ seven years old. His brother Yitz is only

_____. Yitz likes to come to the bus stop to _____

Dovid's bus. When Yitz sees the big _____ bus

coming down the road he begins to _____ up and down. He

gets really excited!

One day as _____ bus rode down his block Dovid turned to

_____ out the window. He did _____ see his brother

Yitz! He began to feel alarmed. Maybe something is not ok. Dovid

got off the bus and quickly walked home. When he got inside he saw

Yitz sleeping on the couch .

He _____ to Yitz in a very quiet voice,"_____ missed

you today! You did not come to see _____ get off my bus."

He gave Yitz a big kiss on his soft cheek.

Spelling

Name: _____   **Date:** _____

Spelling

short ă and short ĭ words;

1. hand

2. class

3. stamp

4. spin

5. drip

6. wind

Extra Credit;

7. are

8. little

Name: _____   **Date:** _____

Spelling Pre-Test

1. _____

_____

2. _____

_____

3. _____

_____

4. _____

_____

5. _____

_____

6. _____

_____

<u>Extra Credit</u>;

7. _____

_____

8. _____

_____

Name: _____   **Date:** _____

Spelling Review Sheet

Word Box

hand   class   stamp   wind   spin   drip   are   little

Fill in the missing word;

1. Do you write with your left or right _____?

2. The strong _____ blew my hat off my head.

3. Where _____ you going for vacation?

4. My _____ baby sister has one tooth.

5. You need to put a _____ on an envelope in order to

   mail it.

6. The broken sink will _____ water until it gets fixed.

7. Our _____ won the brachos contest.

8. On Chanukah I will _____ the dreidel until I get a

   gimmel.

Name: _____   **Date:** _____

Spelling Review Sheet

Word Box

hand   class   stamp   wind   spin   drip   are   little

Fill in the blanks with words that rhyme from the spelling list.
Then think of your own rhyming words.

Rhyme	Spelling word	Your own rhyme
land		
damp		
skip		
far		
pass		
bin		
middle		
pinned		

Name: _____　　　　　**Date:** _____

Spelling Review Sheet

Word Box

hand　class　stamp　wind　spin　drip　are　little

Correct the spelling mistakes.

1. The Rebbe gave me a **stap** on my paper for good work.

   _____

2. There **ar** twenty eight boys in my **clas**. _____

   _____

3. I use my right **hannd** to cover my eyes when I say shema.

   _____

4. We have two **liddel** menorahs for the younger children.

   _____

5. During the big storm the strong **wend** blew down many trees.

   _____

6. If you **sipn** on a shin you will have to put one in.

   _____

7. Do not **jrip** water all over the floor when you wash your hands.

Name: _____   **Date:** _____

Up the Hill

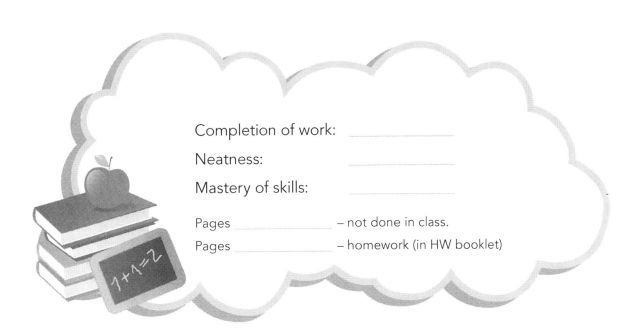

Completion of work: _____

Neatness: _____

Mastery of skills: _____

Pages _____ – not done in class.

Pages _____ – homework (in HW booklet)

**Grade: 2
Volume: 10**

Parents signature: _____

Reading

Name: _____ **Date:** _____

Up the Hill

press the pedal

Fran, Dennis, and Moppet

in the wagon

"I can't get the car to the top,"...

Moppet pulled

a grand trip

Name: _____   Date: _____

Up the Hill

Dennis has a car.

It is red.

His car can go fast.

To start his car, Dennis has to press the pedal.

It is after supper.

Fran, Dennis, and Moppet sit on the steps.

"Let's go up the hill," said Dennis.

"No, I want to rest," said Fran.

Dennis said, "You sit in the wagon.

I will get in the car.

The car will pull you.

You can rest and still go up the hill."

Dennis got in the car.

Fran got in the wagon and held on.

Moppet ran up to her.

"Arf, arf," he said.

"Moppet wants to get in the wagon," said Fran

Name: _____   **Date:** _____

"Well, tell him he can't get in," said Dennis.

"I can't pull you and Moppet."

Dennis pressed the pedal. The car started up the hill. U...p, u...p went the car. It stopped.

"I can't get the car to the top," said Dennis.

Moppet ran up the hill to Fran.

"Arf, arf," he said.

"Moppet wants to help," said Fran.

"He wants to pull us up the hill."

Moppet pulled the car and the wagon.

He got to the top of the hill.

"Arf, arf," said Moppet.

"He wants to get in the wagon," said Fran.

"Tell him he can get in now," said Dennis.

Moppet got in.

"Let's go!" called Fran.

Moppet had a grand trip.

Name: _____　　　**Date:** _____

Story Mapping

Characters	Setting

What happened?

_____

_____

_____

_____

At the end...

_____

_____

Phonics

Name: _____   **Date:** _____

Sort the words on the bottom of the page by syllables.

One Syllable	Two Syllable
fast	Dennis

Dennis	fast	press	pedal
after	supper	Fran	wagon
Moppet	can't	pull	started

Circle the words that are names of characters. What is different about those words? _____

Name: _____   **Date:** _____

Blending Sheet

a	b	c	d	e	f	
g	h	i	j	k	l	
m	n	o	p	q	r	s
t	u	v	w	x	y	z

Name: _____   **Date:** _____

hill

will

sell

swell

tall

fall

small

call

pull

full

1. Underline the vowel in each word- and say the vowel sound. If there are two syllables read one at a time.

2. Read from the vowel till the end.

3. Read the whole word.

Circle the words that need a double ll at the end.

mail	fil	spel
feel	little	ful
bel	bowl	bil
school	peel	pail

Name: _____   **Date:** _____

Sight Word Review

Use the sight words to fill in the missing words.

three	on	do	at
up	to	they	must
be	we	two	with

My baby brother is _____ years old. He has long black hair

that he wears in a pony. His birthday is _____ Chanukah. He will

have a very big birthday party because he is turning _____.

He will _____ getting his first haircut! The party will be

_____ my house. My grandfathers will snip some of his hair first.

Then my father will _____ the rest of the haircut.

In the morning _____ will take him _____ my school. He will

be all wrapped _____ in a tallis. I will show everyone where the

kindergarten classroom is. I will tell everyone that in my school we

_____ be very quiet. We cannot disturb the learning there. He

will sit on the rebbe's lap and say the letters of the aleph bais together

_____ the class. After every letter he will get to lick some honey.

Then he will dance with the rebbe and all the kids in the class. Finally

_____ will each get a party bag with nosh and prizes. I can't wait!

Spelling

Name: _____   **Date:** _____

Spelling

short ĭ words and final double ll;

1. hill

2. will

3. fill

4. still

5. mill

6. till

Extra Credit;

7. all

8. call

Name: _____   **Date:** _____

Spelling Pre-Test

1. _____

_____

2. _____

_____

3. _____

_____

4. _____

_____

5. _____

_____

6. _____

_____

Extra Credit;

7. _____

_____

8. _____

_____

Name: _____   **Date:** _____

Spelling Review Sheet

> Word Box
>
> hill   will   fill   still   mill   till   all   call

Fill in the missing word;

1. Wheat kernels are ground into flour at the _____.

2. My friend lives at the top of a big _____.

3. My class _____ have a siyum when we finish the parsha.

4. I like to _____ my bubby on the telephone every Friday to say good shabbos.

5. It takes a long time to _____ our bathtub with water.

6. _____ the kids in my class will be invited to my birthday party.

7. There is _____ three more weeks left before my party.

8. The bus driver does not drive _____ all the boys are sitting down.

Name: _____   **Date:** _____

Spelling Review Sheet

> Word Box
>
> hill   will   fill   still   mill   till   all   call

Change one letter in each word to find the spelling word. Then change one more letter to make another new word.

Word	Spelling word	Your own word
well		
hull		
stall		
fell		
ill		
ball		
tell		
mall		

Name: _____   **Date:** _____

Spelling Review Sheet

Word Box

hill   will   fill   still   mill   till   all   call

Correct the spelling mistakes.

1. I like to walk up a steep **hil**. _____

2. It **wil** be hard work for my legs. _____

3. I like to watch the wheat kernels turn into flour at the **mil**.

_____

4. At the Kiddush I will **fil** my pockets with candy to take home.

_____

5. My little brother cannot sit **stel** in shul for more than 1 minute.

_____

6. Our class cannot go outside today **tull** we finish the page.

_____

7. **Awl** the boys in the eighth grade will go on an overnight trip.

_____

8. The nurse will **cawl** us in when it is our turn. _____

Name: _____   **Date:** _____

Downtown to the Tower

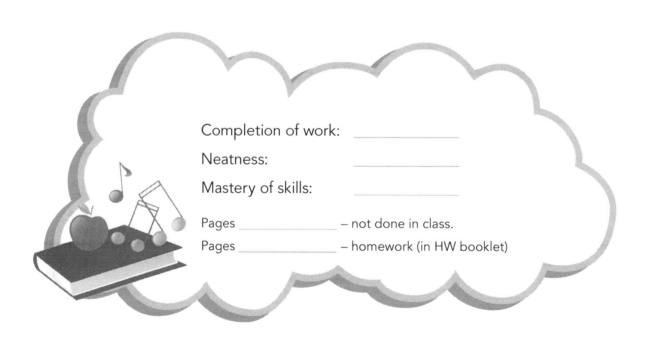

Completion of work: _____

Neatness: _____

Mastery of skills: _____

Pages _____ – not done in class.

Pages _____ – homework (in HW booklet)

Grade: 2
Volume: 11

Parents signature: _____

Reading

Name: _____

Date: _____

Downtown to the Tower

Papa and I went downtown.

tall apartments

papa frowned

tugged hard at us

"See how small the crowd is now!"

on a map

Name: _____   **Date:** _____

Downtown to the Tower

Papa and I went downtown.

We wanted to see the tower.

I wanted to go up to the top of it.

We passed tall apartments.

We saw crowds and lots of cars.

Papa frowned.

"It's too crowded," he said.

"I will stop the car and we can get out."

Papa and I stepped into the crowds.

We stopped at a flower stand.

We saw flags flap in the wind.

We saw a clown in a tall hat.

She put a crown on me.

At last we saw the tower.

It had tall, tall walls of glass.

"I can't see the top of the tower," I said.

Name: _____   **Date:** _____

Papa and I went up, up, up.

"We are at the top now," said Papa.

The wind tugged hard at us.

I held Papa's hand.

From the top we saw downtown and the water, too.

"See how small the crowd is now!" said Papa.

He showed me a map of downtown.

I saw it all from the top of the tower.

"Wow!" I said to Papa.

"It's fun to go up and see down."

Name: _____   **Date:** _____

Story Mapping

Characters	Setting

What happened?

_____

_____

_____

_____

At the end...

_____

_____

Phonics

Name: _____   **Date:** _____

Sort the words on the bottom of the page by syllables.

One Syllable	Two Syllable	Three Syllable
passed	downtown	

downtown	Papa	wanted	tower
passed	apartments	crowds	frowned
crowded	stopped	flower	tugged

Circle the words that are names of characters. What is different about those words? _____

Name: _____   **Date:** _____

Blending Sheet

a	b	c	d	e	f	
g	h	i	j	k	l	
m	n	o	p	q	r	s
t	u	v	w	x	y	z

Name: _____   **Date:** _____

____ n<u>ow</u>

____ cow

____ crowd

____ crowded

____ clown

____ crown

____ drown

_1_ frown

____ flower

____ tower

1. Underline the ow in each word and <u>read it</u>.

2. Read from the <u>ow till the end</u>.

3. Add the <u>beginning</u>.

4. Read the <u>whole word</u>.

Read the clues below. Match them to the words on the left. Write the numbers.

1. The opposite of a smile is a _____.

2. A rose is a type of _____.

3. A lot of people together is a _____.

4. It is _____ when there is not much empty space.

5. A kosher animal that gives us milk is a _____.

6. A king will wear a _____ on his head.

7. A very tall building can be called a _____.

8. Not before, not later, but right _____!

9. If someone's head goes under water for too long they can _____, chas vesholom.

Name: _____   Date: _____

Sight Word Review

Use the sight words to fill in the missing words.

pretty	black	like	get
He	Now	new	have
so	too	well	saw

Yitzchok was sick. _____ did not feel _____. His mom said, "I will take you to see Dr. Wong."

Dr. Wong is nice and funny," said Yitzchok. "I _____ her."

When Yitzchok and his mom went to the doctor's office they _____ a different doctor. It was not Dr. Wong.

"Where is Dr. Wong?" asked Yitzchok.

"She is sick. I am Dr. Stevens. I am a doctor who helps Dr. Wong. Tell me what feels bad, _____ that I can help you feel better."

"My throat hurts and I cough a lot _____," said Yitzchok.

Dr. Stevens took out a _____ otoscope to check his ears. Then he looked into Yitzchok's throat and said, "Your ears and throat do not look _____! They are infected. You will need to take medicine for ten days."

Dr. Stevens gave Yitzchok a _____ box of crayons for a prize. "You were a really brave young man," he said. "Feel better!"

"_____ we will go _____ medicine from the pharmacy," said Mom. "Thank you Dr. Stevens, and _____ a good day."

Spelling

Name: _____   **Date:** _____

Spelling

short ĕ words;

1. leg

- -

2. men

- -

3. bend

- -

4. went

- -

5. tent

- -

6. web

- -

Extra Credit;

7. number

- -

8. you

Name: _____   **Date:** _____

Spelling Pre-Test

1. _____

2. _____

3. _____

4. _____

5. _____

6. _____

Extra Credit;

7. _____

8. _____

Name: _____   **Date:** _____

Spelling Review Sheet

Word Box

leg   men   went   tent   bend   web   you   number

Fill in the missing word;

1. A spider _____ once saved Dovid Hamelech.

2. Most tables stand on four _____ s.

3. When we have more than one man we call them _____.

4. "Where are _____ going?" the little boy asked his mother.

5. Last shabbos we _____ to a Kiddush.

6. If you go camping you can sleep in a _____.

7. It is hard for my grandmother to _____ down.

8. It is important for a child to know his phone _____.

Name: _____   **Date:** _____

Spelling Review Sheet

Word Box

leg   men   went   tent   bend   web   you   number

Fill in the spelling word (or words) that rhyme. Can you add your own?

Word	Spelling word	Your own word
spend		
lumber		
sent		
peg		
pen		
shoe		
Reb		

Name: _____   **Date:** _____

Spelling Review Sheet

Word Box

leg   men   went   tent   bend   web   you   number

Correct the spelling mistakes.

1. I hurt my **legg** when I fell off my bike. _____

2. Avrohom Avinu had a four door **tant**. _____

3. The bug got stuck in the spider's **wed**? _____

4. I am looking for the house **nummer** 75 on my block.

_____

5. **Yu** are an excellent student. _____

6. I **band** down and touch my toes when I do exercise.

_____

7. There are two **man** fixing the street in front of my house.

_____

Name: _____

Date: _____

The Smartest Batter

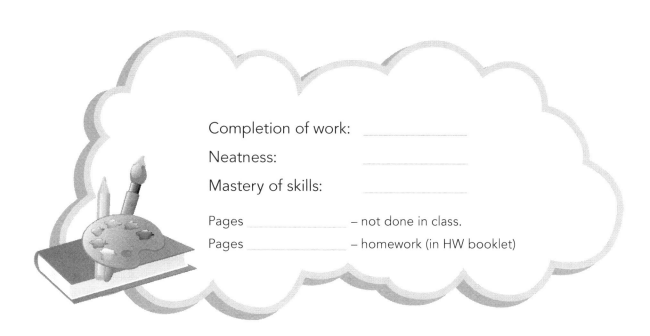

Completion of work: _____

Neatness: _____

Mastery of skills: _____

Pages _____ – not done in class.

Pages _____ – homework (in HW booklet)

Grade: 2
Volume: 12

Parents signature: _____

Reading

Name: _____   Date: _____

The Smartest Batter

Better Batter Ball Club

bats well and runs fast

Bob spotted the ball

into the pig pen

hollered and clapped

the smartest members

Name: _____   **Date:** _____

The Smartest Batter

Bob is on Mr. Wilson's ball club.

The club is called the 3-Bs.

The 3-Bs stands for Better Batter Ball Club.

Bob's pals go to the club, too.

They go to Mr. Wilson's farm in a bus.

Bob is not a bad hitter.

He bats well and runs fast.

But his pal, Len, is better.

Len is the best hitter on the club.

Last summer, Len hit a ball hard.

The ball went past Mr. Wilson's cows.

It went past Mr. Wilson's garden.

Bob missed the ball.

It landed far up the hill.

Bob had to run after it.

At last the ball stopped.

It stopped in Mr. Wilson's pig pen.

Name: _____   **Date:** _____

Bob spotted the ball in the pen.

But he had a problem.

The pen was full of big pigs.

The biggest pig saw the ball.

The pig grabbed it.

Bob must not go into the pig pen.

How will he get the ball?

Bob ran fast to Mr. Wilson's garden.

He pulled up a carrot and ran to the pig pen.

The big pig still had the ball.

Bob held the carrot in front of the pig.

It dropped the ball and grabbed the carrot.

Bob grabbed the ball and held it up.

The 3-Bs hollered and clapped.

Len is the best batter.

But Bob is the smartest member of the Better Batter Ball Club.

Name: _____   **Date:** _____

Story Mapping

Characters	Setting
_____	_____
_____	_____
_____	_____
_____	_____
_____	_____

What happened?

_____

_____

_____

_____

_____

At the end...

_____

_____

Phonics

Name: _____   **Date:** _____

Sort the words on the bottom of the page by syllables.

One Syllable	Two Syllable
club	smartest

smartest	batter	better	ball
club	Wilson	farm	hitter
summer	garden	missed	landed

Circle the words that are names of characters. What is different about those words? _____

Name: _____   Date: _____

Blending Sheet

a	b	c	d	e	f	
g	h	i	j	k	l	
m	n	o	p	q	r	s
t	u	v	w	x	y	z

Name: _____   **Date:** _____

Match the words on the right with a phrase on the left.
Write the letters.

(a) bus

(b) barn

(c) bottom

(d) better

(e) biggest

(f) bigger

(g) batter

(h) best

(i) number

(j) member

_a_ it can be yellow

___ the opposite of top

___ more big

___ the most big

___ a small red house

___ someone who bats

___ the most good

___ more good

___ part of a group

___ 100,000

Name: _____   **Date:** _____

Sight Word Review

Use the sight words to fill in the missing words.

good	ate	into	did
ride	four	came	yes
went	white	He	want

Today my class _____ to the zoo. We got to _____

on a big, yellow bus. When we got to the zoo the teacher said, "You

must be _____ and follow the rules." We said, "_____!

We will be good!"

My favorite animal was the polar bear. His fur was _____.

He swam in the water and _____ up close to us. He even

_____ some tricks with a ball! Then the zoo keeper fed him

four fish. He _____ all _____ fish. _____

was hungry!

At the end of the day we went _____ a small house with

tables and chairs. We had snacks and drinks. I had fun at the zoo! I

_____ to go back to the zoo again sometime.

Spelling

B
A
C

Name: _____   **Date:** _____

Spelling

short ŏ words;

1. lock

2. clock

3. sock

4. block

5. dock

6. from

Extra Credit;

7. soft

8. pocket

Name: _____   **Date:** _____

Spelling Pre-Test

1. _____

2. _____

3. _____

4. _____

5. _____

6. _____

Extra Credit;

7. _____

8. _____

Name: _____   **Date:** _____

Spelling Review Sheet

Word Box

lock   clock   sock   block   dock   from   soft   pocket

Fill in the missing word;

1. The opposite of hard is _____.

2. A _____ tells us what time it is.

3. When we don't want someone to come in we _____
   the door.

4. My father keeps his phone in his _____.

5. My cousin lives on my _____.

6. I am missing one black _____.

7. We waited on the _____ until it was our turn to go on
   the boat.

8. My mother comes _____ Eretz Yisroel.

Name: _____   Date: _____

Spelling Review Sheet

Word Box

lock   clock   sock   block   dock   from   soft   pocket

Change one letter to make a word from the spelling list. Then try to make another new word of your own.

word	spelling word	your own word
lick		
sift		
packet		
sack		
duck		
frog		
click		

Name: _____   **Date:** _____

Spelling Review Sheet

Word Box

lock   clock   sock   block   dock   from   soft   pocket

Correct the spelling mistakes.

1. We have a combination **lok** at our house. _____

2. I can tell time on a big **klok**. _____

3. I got mud in my **sack** from the backyard? _____

4. My sister got a prize **frum** her teacher. _____

5. I like to play with **blacks**. _____

6. The boat was next to the **dok** by the lake. _____

7. The cake was very **sooft**. _____

Writing
Second Grade

Name: _____   **Date:** _____

Writing Program: Second Grade

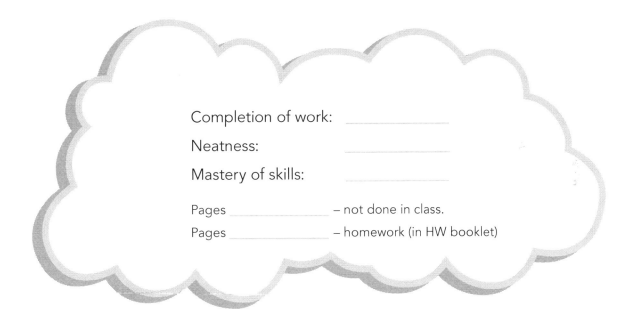

Completion of work: _____

Neatness: _____

Mastery of skills: _____

Pages _____ – not done in class.

Pages _____ – homework (in HW booklet)

Part 1

Parents signature: _____

Name: _____   Date: _____

Lesson 1: Grouping

Complete the groups by choosing the picture at the end that belongs with the others.

Name: _____   **Date:** _____

Complete the groups by choosing the best picture at the end. Then name the group.

1.

school

2.

_____

3.

_____

4.

_____

snacks   farm animals   games   school

Name: _____   **Date:** _____

Complete the groups by choosing the best word at the end. Then name the group.

1. New York	**New Jersey**	**California**	<u>**Texas**</u>	**Yankel**
_____ states _____				
2. Yitzchok	**Yosef**	**Yisroel**	**Batsheva**	**Chaim**
_____				
3. river	**ocean**	**lake**	**sea**	**park**
_____				
4. Yehudis	**Rochel**	**Rivky**	**Hershel**	**Devorah**
_____				
5. USA	**Mexico**	**England**	**Canada**	**Lakewood**
_____				
6. car	**bus**	**train**	**boat**	**fish**
_____				

countries	bodies of water	forms of transportation
girl names	boy names	states

Name: _____   **Date:** _____

Read the group name. Complete the group using your own ideas.

Insects
ants
spiders

Wild Animals
lion
zebra

Fish
salmon
tuna

Pets
dog
goldfish

Local Animals
squirrels
birds

Name: _____   **Date:** _____

Read the group name. Complete the group using your own ideas.

Breakfast

scrambled eggs

_____

Lunch

tuna sandwhich

_____

Supper

meatballs and spaghetti

_____

Name: _____   **Date:** _____

Read the group name. Complete the group using your own ideas.

Rosh Hashana

_____

_____

_____

Yom Kippur

_____

_____

_____

Succos

_____

_____

_____

Name: _____   **Date:** _____

Lesson 2: Sentences and phrases

> A **sentence** tells a complete thought. (who and what)
>
> A **phrase** is a group of words that do not tell a complete thought.

Look at the picture and read the words below it.

Circle the words that tell a complete thought (sentence).

Tim sees
Tim sees the ball.

having fun
Panda is having fun.

The leaves fall off the trees.
off the trees

the cute baby
The baby is sleeping.

Name: _____   **Date:** _____

Circle the words that are a sentence. Then write the sentence on the line.

1. <u>We had chicken for supper.</u>   chicken for supper

_____

_____

2. I like chicken cutlets better.   chicken cutlets

_____

_____

3. Rice and mushrooms.   My mom served rice and mushrooms too.

_____

_____

4. First she served us soup.   she served

_____

_____

5. I like chicken cutlets better.   the chicken

_____

_____

Name: _____   **Date:** _____

Combine the phrases to form one complete sentence.

The ice cream	is very hot.
My best friend	in Lakewood.
I live	it will rain.
The chicken soup	is very cold.
In the morning	is Zevi.

Choose a sentence from above and write it on the line.

_____

_____

_____

_____

Name: _____   **Date:** _____

Lesson 3: Sentence Punctuation

<u>Beginning a Sentence</u>

Read each sentence. Underline the first letter of each sentence.

1. <u>A</u> dog is a good pet.

2. My dog can run fast.

3. Rags can play ball.

4. Rags can jump.

5. Do you want a pet?

6. I will give you a pup.

Rewrite the following sentences on. Don't forget to capitalize the first word in every sentence.

1. the sun is hot.

_____

_____

2. we will go home.

_____

_____

3. you can come with us.

_____

_____

4. we will get some water.

_____

Name: _____   **Date:** _____

Ending a Telling Sentence

Insert the proper end punctuation. Then rewrite the sentences on the bottom.

1. Bob has a book (.)
2. The book is old ( )
3. Bob likes his book ( )
4. It is a good book ( )
5. I want to read it ( )
6. It is about bugs ( )

7. This is my home

_____

- -

_____

8. I cut the grass

_____

- -

_____

9. Next, I rake it

_____

- -

_____

10. It looks good

_____

Name: _____   **Date:** _____

Lesson 4: Sentence Order

Circle the sentence that makes sense. Then write the sentence on the line.

1. <u>Max runs home.</u>   Runs Max home.

_____

_____

2. Plays he ball.   He plays ball.

_____

_____

3. Mom late is.   Mom is late.

_____

_____

4. Come here she.   Here she comes.

_____

_____

5. Mom plays, too.   Too plays Mom.

_____

_____

Name: _____   **Date:** _____

Circle the sentence that makes sense. Then write the sentence on the line.

1. Fun they have.   <u>They have fun.</u>

_____

2. Then they eat.   Eat then they.

_____

3. Sleeps Max next.   Next, Max sleeps.

_____

4. Seven am I.   I am seven.

_____

5. We are happy.   Happy are we.

_____

Name: _____   **Date:** _____

Write each sentence in correct order.

1. fast Jim swims.

Jim swims fast.

2. cannot swim I.

3. math likes Pinny.

4. Moishy art likes.

5. to town Eva walks.

Name: _____   **Date:** _____

Underline the group of words that are a proper sentence.

1. <u>Amy stands still.</u>   Amy still

2. She feeds   She feeds the deer.

3. The deer is not afraid.   not afraid

4. Amy's hand   It eats from Amy's hand.

Rewrite these sentences in the proper order.

1. pets the Amy deer.

_____

_____

2. deer is The soft.

_____

_____

3. Its cold nose is.

_____

_____

4. Scared gets The deer.

_____

_____

5. leaves deer The.

_____

_____

Name: _____   **Date:** _____

Lesson 5: Telling Sentences

Yanky is telling his class about his trip. This is what he said.

(Read the sentences that Yanky said and write them over on the lines.)

1. I went on a trip to _____(the country).

_____

_____

2. I went swimming.

_____

_____

3. I saw some animals.

_____

_____

4. I found a frog.

_____

_____

5. Dad took pictures.

_____

_____

Name: _____   **Date:** _____

6. We had a picnic.

_____
- -
_____

7. It was fun.

_____
- -
_____

8. I liked my trip.

_____
- -
_____

Complete the following writing activity by writing telling sentences. Draw a picture of your trip on the title page. Then write four sentences telling about your trip.

Name: _____   **Date:** _____

By: _____

Name: _____   **Date:** _____

We went on a trip to

Name: _____   **Date:** _____

Lesson 6: Asking Sentences

Yanky just met Chaim. He is asking him questions. Read the questions he asks. Write them over on the lines. Be sure to make a question mark at the end of every asking sentence.

1. What is your name?

_____

_____

2. When is your birthday?

_____

_____

3. Where do you live?

_____

_____

4. How old are you?

_____

_____

Name: _____   **Date:** _____

5. Who lives with you?

_____

- -

_____

6. Did you meet my sister?

_____

- -

_____

7. Why do you have a ball?

_____

- -

_____

Here are some asking words, words that begin an asking sentence.

who - what - when - where - why - how

Name: _____   **Date:** _____

<u>Ending a Telling Sentence</u>

1. Who is here ⊘

2. When will it be time to go ◯

3. Will we go soon ◯

4. Do you have your coat ◯

5. Where is my coat ◯

6. Who is going with us ◯

7. Who said my name

_____

_____

8. Was it Bud

_____

_____

9. Did Bud go home

_____

_____

10. When will he come back

_____

Name: _____   **Date:** _____

Here are some asking words, words that begin an asking sentence.

who - what - when - where - why - how

Write an asking sentence about each picture. Use one of the asking words above to start your sentence.

Example;  Where are my shoes?

1. _____
   _____
   _____

2. _____
   _____
   _____

3. _____
   _____
   _____

Name: _____   **Date:** _____

Read and copy the sentences below. Draw a circle around the number before the sentence if it is an asking sentence. Draw a box around the number if it is a telling sentence.

1. I see a kite.

_____

_____

2. Is it for me?

_____

_____

3. We can fly the kite.

_____

_____

4. Will you race me?

_____

_____

5. Can you go fast?

_____

_____

Name: _____   **Date:** _____

6. Ben has my kite.

_____

- -

_____

7. Is the sun hot?

_____

- -

_____

8. Write a telling sentence. Tell about something you do in school.

Example: I read and write in school.

_____

- -

_____

9. Write an asking sentence. Ask your mother a question.

Example: Can I have a cookie please?

_____

- -

_____

Name: _____   **Date:** _____

Review End Punctuation

<u>Ending Sentences . or ?</u>

1. It will rain all day (.)

2. Where can we have a picnic ◯

3. We can have it on the porch ◯

4. You and I will make the food ◯

5. What food do you like ◯

6. I like hot dogs ◯

7. Who will get the chairs ◯

8. Who will sit next to me ◯

9. Tom will sit next to me ◯

10. We will play games ◯

11. Who will win ◯

12. When will the sun shine ◯

Name: _____   **Date:** _____

Lesson 7: Writing project using telling sentences

Place a picture of your family here!

....

By: _____

Name: _____   **Date:** _____

Use telling sentences to tell about your father.

<u>My Father</u>

1. Tell one thing that your father does every day.

_____

_____

_____

2. Tell one thing that you do with your father.

_____

_____

_____

3. Tell one thing that you have to thank your father for.

_____

_____

_____

4. What is something that you learned from your father?

_____

_____

_____

5. Write a sentence telling how you feel about your father.

_____

_____

_____

Name: _____   **Date:** _____

Draw a picture to describe at least one of the sentences telling about your father.

<u>**My Father**</u>

_____

_ _

_____

_____

_ _

_____

_____

_ _

_____

_____

_ _

Name: _____   **Date:** _____

Use telling sentences to tell about your mother.

<u>My Mother</u>

1. Tell one thing that your mother does every day.

_____

- -

_____

2. Tell one thing that your mother does every Friday.

_____

- -

_____

3. Tell one thing that you have to thank your mother for.

_____

- -

_____

4. What is something that you learned from your mother?

_____

- -

_____

5. Write a sentence telling how you feel about your mother.

_____

- -

_____

Name: _____   **Date:** _____

Draw a picture to describe at least one of the sentences telling about your mother.

<u>**My Mother**</u>

Name: _____   **Date:** _____

Use telling sentences to tell about your brothers and sisters.

<u>My brothers and sisters</u>

1. How many brothers and sisters do you have in your family?

_____

_____

_____

2. What is your place in the family? (oldest, youngest, middle)

_____

_____

_____

3. What is your favorite thing to do with your sisters and brothers?

_____

_____

_____

4. How can you be a better brother to your siblings?

_____

_____

_____

5. Write a sentence telling how you feel about your sisters and brothers.

_____

_____

_____

_____

Name: _____   **Date:** _____

Draw a picture to describe at least one of the sentences telling about your sisters and brothers.

<u>**My Sisters and Brothers**</u>

_____

_____

_____

_____

_____

_____

_____

Name: _____   **Date:** _____

Lesson 8: Asking Sentences

Yanky just met Chaim. He is asking him questions. Read the questions he asked. Write them over on the lines. Be sure to make a question mark at the end of every asking sentence.

1. What is your name?

_____

- -

_____

2. When is your birthday?

_____

- -

_____

3. Where do you live?

_____

- -

_____

4. How old are you?

_____

- -

_____

Name: _____   **Date:** _____

5. Who lives with you?

_____

- -

_____

6. Did you meet my sister?

_____

- -

_____

7. Why do you have a ball?

_____

- -

_____

Use the writing activity on the next page to practice writing telling sentences.

First place a picture of yourself in the box on the title page. Then complete the telling sentences in the box on the next page. Finally write the sentences over on the lines. Don't forget to put a period at the end of every telling sentence.

Name: _____   **Date:** _____

Lesson 9: Writing project using telling sentences

All About Me

Put a picture of yourself here.

_____

By: _____

Name: _____   **Date:** _____

My name is _____.

My birthday is on _____.

I live at _____.

I am _____ years old.

I go to _____.

I like to play _____.

My favorite food is _____.

I am good at _____.

_____

_____

_____

_____

_____

Name: _____ **Date:** _____

Name: _____   **Date:** _____

Lesson 10: Naming Part of Sentences

Each sentence has a naming part that names someone or something. Read each sentence and the question below it. Then write the answer to the question.

1. Rick went to the zoo.

Who did something? _____

2. The monkey did some tricks.

What did something? _____

3. The bear ate some food.

What did something? _____

4. The lions roared.

What did something? _____

Name: _____   **Date:** _____

5. The tiger slept in its cage.

_____

What did something? _____

6. Sue rode on an elephant.

_____

Who did something? _____

7. The pink birds ran together.

_____

What did something? _____

8. The turtle swam in the water.

_____

What did something? _____

Name: _____   Date: _____

Lesson 11: Action Part of Sentences

Read the naming part of each sentence. Complete the sentence by writing an action part from the box.

> ate the food.
>
> fed the dog.
>
> helped Dan.

Dan _____ .

The dog _____ .

I _____ .

Name: _____   **Date:** _____

Read the action part of each sentence. Complete the sentence by writing a naming part from the box.

> **The bird**
>
> **Many friends**
>
> **Pat**

_____ has a new bird.

_____ is very small.

_____ come to see it.

Name: _____   **Date:** _____

Read each sentence and write T if the sentence is a telling sentence and A if the sentence is an asking sentence.

_____ 1. Did you go to the park?

_____ 2. Yes, we went to the park.

_____ 3. Was the park full?

_____ 4. The park was not full.

_____ 5. Are the rides scary?

_____ 6. Some rides are scary.

_____ 7. Did you have fun?

_____ 8. We had a great time.

Match naming parts with action parts to form complete sentences. Write the sentences on the lines.

The children	has many rides.
The park	can be scary.
Some rides	went to the park.

1. _____

   _____

2. _____

   _____

3. _____

   _____

Name: _____   **Date:** _____

Read the naming parts and the action parts in the boxes. Use these sentence parts to write a story about your school.

My school	reads books.
My teacher	likes me.
Our class	is fun.
My friend	is big.
Our playground	takes us places.
The bus	is happy.
Our room	looks nice.

My Story

1. _____

2. _____

3. _____

4. _____

5. _____

6. _____

7. _____

8. _____

Made in the USA
Middletown, DE
12 April 2023

28725707R00121